Depression and Anxiety

Bhaskar Pandey

Social media connectivity

INSTAGRAM@ <u>DEAD_OF_WRITE27</u>
@ <u>INK_AND_FABLES27</u>
@ <u>VINTAGE_QUOTES_WORDS</u>
TWITTER@ <u>BHASKAR_PANDEY</u>

Everything You Need to Know About Anxiety

Overview

Anxiety is your body's natural response to stress. It's a feeling of fear or apprehension about what's to come. The first day of school, going to a job interview, or giving a speech may

cause most people to feel fearful
and nervous.

But if your feelings of anxiety
are extreme, last for longer than
six months, and are interfering
with your life, you may have an
anxiety disorder.

What are anxiety disorders?

It's normal to feel anxious about
moving to a new place, starting a
new job, or taking a test. This
type of anxiety is unpleasant,
but it may motivate you to work
harder and to do a better job.

Ordinary anxiety is a feeling
that comes and goes, but does not
interfere with your everyday
life.

In the case of an anxiety
disorder, the feeling of fear may
be with you all the time. It is
intense and sometimes
debilitating.

This type of anxiety may cause
you to stop doing things you
enjoy. In extreme cases, it may
prevent you from entering an
elevator, crossing the street, or
even leaving your home. If left

untreated, the anxiety will keep
getting worse.

Anxiety disorders are the most
common form of emotional disorder
and can affect anyone at any age.
According to the American
Psychiatric Association, women
are more likely than men to be
diagnosed with an anxiety
disorder.

What are the types of anxiety disorders?

Anxiety is a key part of several
different disorders. These
include:

- panic disorder: experiencing
  recurring panic attacks at
  unexpected times. A person
  with panic disorder may live
  in fear of the next panic
  attack.
- phobia: excessive fear of a
  specific object, situation,
  or activity
- social anxiety disorder:
  extreme fear of being judged
  by others in social
  situations
- obsessive-compulsive
  disorder: recurring

irrational thoughts that lead
you to perform specific,
repeated behaviors
* separation anxiety disorder:
fear of being away from home
or loved ones
* illness anxiety disorder:
anxiety about your health
(formerly called
hypochondria)
* post-traumatic stress
disorder (PTSD): anxiety
following a traumatic event

What are the symptoms of anxiety?

Anxiety feels different depending on the person experiencing it. Feelings can range from butterflies in your stomach to a racing heart. You might feel out of control, like there's a disconnect between your mind and body.

Other ways people experience anxiety include nightmares, panic attacks, and painful thoughts or memories that you can't control.

You may have a general feeling of
fear and worry, or you may fear a
specific place or event.

Symptoms of general anxiety
include:

- increased heart rate
- rapid breathing
- restlessness
- trouble concentrating
- difficulty falling asleep

Your anxiety symptoms might be
totally different from someone
else's. That's why it's important
to know all the ways anxiety can
present itself.

What is an anxiety attack?

An anxiety attack is a feeling of overwhelming apprehension, worry, distress, or fear. For many people, an anxiety attack builds slowly. It may worsen as a stressful event approaches.

Anxiety attacks can vary greatly, and symptoms may differ among individuals. That's because the many symptoms of anxiety don't happen to everyone, and they can change over time.

Common symptoms of an anxiety
attack include:

- feeling faint or dizzy
- shortness of breath
- dry mouth
- sweating
- chills or hot flashes
- apprehension and worry
- restlessness
- distress
- fear
- numbness or tingling

A panic attack and an anxiety
attack share some common
symptoms, but they're not the
same.

What causes anxiety?

Researchers are not sure of the exact cause of anxiety. But, it's likely a combination of factors play a role. These include genetic and environmental factors, as well as brain chemistry.

In addition, researchers believe that the areas of the brain responsible for controlling fear may be impacted.

Current research of anxiety is taking a deeper look at the parts of the brain that are involved with anxiety.

Are there tests that diagnose anxiety?

A single test can't diagnose anxiety. Instead, an anxiety diagnosis requires a lengthy process of physical examinations, mental health evaluations, and psychological questionnaires.

Some doctors may conduct a physical exam, including blood or urine tests to rule out underlying medical conditions that could contribute to symptoms you're experiencing.

Several anxiety tests and scales are also used to help your doctor assess the level of anxiety you're experiencing. Reach about each of these tests.

What are treatments for anxiety?

Once you've been diagnosed with anxiety, you can to explore treatment options with your doctor. For some people, medical treatment isn't necessary. Lifestyle changes may be enough to cope with the symptoms.

In moderate or severe cases, however, treatment can help you overcome the symptoms and lead a more manageable day-to-day life.

Treatment for anxiety falls into two categories: psychotherapy and medication. Meeting with a therapist or psychologist can help you learn tools to use and

strategies to cope with anxiety
when it occurs.

Medications typically used to
treat anxiety include
antidepressants and sedatives.
They work to balance brain
chemistry, prevent episodes of
anxiety, and ward off the most
severe symptoms of the disorder.

What natural remedies are

used for anxiety?

Lifestyle changes can be an effective way to relieve some of the stress and anxiety you may cope with every day. Most of the natural "remedies" consist of caring for your body, participating in healthy activities, and eliminating unhealthy ones.

These include:

- getting enough sleep
- meditating

- staying active and exercising
- eating a healthy diet
- staying active and working out
- avoiding alcohol
- avoiding caffeine
- quitting smoking cigarettes

If these lifestyle changes seem like a positive way to help you eliminate some anxiety, read about how each one works—plus, get more great ideas for treating anxiety.

Anxiety and depression

If you have an anxiety disorder,
you may also be depressed. While
anxiety and depression can occur
separately, it's not unusual for
these to mental health disorders
to happen together.

Anxiety can be a symptom of
clinical or major depression.
Likewise, worsening symptoms of
depression can be triggered by an
anxiety disorder.

Symptoms of both conditions can
be managed with many of the same
treatments: psychotherapy
(counselling), medications, and
lifestyle changes.

How to help children with anxiety

Anxiety in children is natural and common. In fact, one in eight children will experience anxiety. As children grow up and learn from their parents, friends, and caretakers, they typically develop the skills to calm themselves and cope with feelings of anxiety.

But, anxiety in children can also become chronic and persistent, developing into an anxiety

disorder. Uncontrolled anxiety
may begin to interfere with daily
activities, and children may
avoid interacting with their
peers or family members.

Symptoms of an anxiety disorder
might include:

- jitteriness
- irritability
- sleeplessness
- feelings of fear
- shame
- feelings of isolation

Anxiety treatment for children
includes cognitive behavioral

therapy (talk therapy) and
medications.

Get Answers from a Doctor in Minutes, Anytime

Have medical questions? Connect
with a board-certified,
experienced doctor online or by
phone. Pediatricians and other
specialists available 24/7

How to help teens with anxiety

Teenagers may have many reasons to be anxious. Tests, college visits, and first dates all pop up in these important years. But teenagers who feel anxious or experience symptoms of anxiety frequently may have an anxiety disorder.

Symptoms of anxiety in teenagers may include nervousness, shyness, isolationist behaviours, and avoidance. Likewise, anxiety in

teens may lead to unusual
behaviours. They may act out,
perform poorly in school, skip
social events, and even engage in
substance or alcohol use.

For some teens, depression may
accompany anxiety. Diagnosing
both conditions is important so
that treatment can address the
underlying issues and help
relieve symptoms.

The most common treatments for
anxiety in teenagers are talk
therapy and medication. These
treatments also help address
depression symptoms.

Anxiety and stress

Stress and anxiety are two sides of the same coin. Stress is the result of demands on your brain or body. It can be the caused by an event or activity that makes you nervous or worrisome. Anxiety is that same worry, fear, or unease.

Anxiety can be a reaction to your stress, but it can also occur in people who have no obvious stressors.

Both anxiety and stress cause
physical and mental symptoms.
These include:

- headache
- stomachache
- fast heartbeat
- sweating
- dizziness
- jitteriness
- muscle tension
- rapid breathing
- panic
- nervousness
- difficulty concentrating
- irrational anger or
  irritability
- restlessness

- sleeplessness

Neither stress nor anxiety is always bad. Both can actually provide you with a bit of a boost or incentive to accomplish the task or challenge before you. However, if they become persistent, they can begin to interfere with your daily life. In that case, it's important to seek treatment.

The long-term outlook for untreated depression and anxiety includes chronic health issues, such as heart disease.

Anxiety and alcohol

If you're anxious frequently, you may decide you'd like a drink to calm your nerves. After all, alcohol is a sedative. It can depress the activity of your central nervous system, which may help you feel more relaxed.

In a social setting, that may feel like just the answer you need to let down your guard. Ultimately, it may not be the best solution.

Some people with anxiety disorders end up abusing alcohol or other drugs in an effort to feel better regularly. This can create dependency and addiction.

It may be necessary to treat an alcohol or drug problem before the anxiety can be addressed. Chronic or long-term use can ultimately make the condition worse, too. Read more to understand how alcohol can make symptoms of anxiety or an anxiety disorder worse.

Can foods treat anxiety?

Medication and talk therapy are commonly used to treat anxiety. Lifestyle changes, like getting enough sleep and regular exercise, can also help. In addition, some research suggests the foods you eat may have a beneficial impact on your brain if you frequently experience anxiety.

These foods include:

- salmon
- chamomile

- turmeric

- dark chocolate

- yogurt

- green tea

Outlook

Anxiety disorders can be treated
with medication, psychotherapy,
or a combination of the two. Some
people who have a mild anxiety
disorder, or a fear of something
they can easily avoid, decide to
live with the condition and do
not seek treatment.

It's important to understand that
anxiety disorders can be treated,

even in severe cases. Although
anxiety usually doesn't go away,
you can learn to manage it and
live a happy, healthy life.

Everything You Want to Know About Depression

What is depression?

Depression is classified as a mood disorder. It may be described as feelings of sadness, loss, or anger that interfere

with a person's everyday
activities.

It's also fairly common. The
Centers for Disease Control and
Prevention (CDC)estimates that
8.1 per cent of American adults
ages 20 and over had depression
in any given two-week period from
2013 to 2016.

People experience depression in
different ways. It may interfere
with your daily work, resulting
in lost time and lower
productivity. It also can
influence relationships and some
chronic health conditions.

Conditions that can get worse due
to depression include:

- arthritis
- asthma
- cardiovascular disease
- cancer
- diabetes
- obesity

It's important to realize that
feeling down at times is a normal
part of life. Sad and upsetting
events happen to everyone. But,
if you're feeling miserable or
hopeless on a regular basis, you
could be dealing with depression.

Depression is considered a serious medical condition, and it can get worse without proper treatment. Yet, those who seek treatment often see improvements in symptoms in just a few weeks.

Depression symptoms

Depression can be more than a constant state of sadness or feeling "blue."

Major depression can cause a variety of symptoms. Some affect your mood, and others affect your

body. Symptoms may also be
ongoing or come and go.

Depression can affect men, women,
and children differently.

Symptoms of depression in men may
include:

- Mood: anger, aggressiveness,
  irritability, anxiousness,
  restlessness
- Emotional: feeling empty,
  sad, hopeless
- Behavioral: loss of interest,
  no longer finding pleasure in
  favourite activities, feeling
  tired easily, thoughts of
  suicide, drinking

excessively, using drugs, engaging in high-risk activities

- Sexual: reduced sexual desire, lack of sexual performance
- Cognitive: inability to concentrate, difficulty completing tasks, delayed responses during conversations
- Sleep: insomnia, restless sleep, excessive sleepiness, not sleeping through the night
- Physical: fatigue, pains, headache, digestive problems

Symptoms of depression in women
may include:

- Mood: irritability
- Emotional: feeling sad or
  empty, anxious or hopeless
- Behavioral: loss of interest
  in activities, withdrawing
  from social engagements,
  thoughts of suicide
- Cognitive: thinking or
  talking more slowly
- Sleep: difficulty sleeping
  through the night, waking
  early, sleeping too much
- Physical: decreased energy,
  greater fatigue, changes in
  appetite, weight changes,

aches, pain, headaches,
increased cramps

Symptoms of depression in
children may include:

- Mood: irritability, anger,
  mood swings, crying
- Emotional: feelings of
  incompetence (e.g. "I can't
  do anything right") or
  despair, crying, intense
  sadness
- Behavioral: getting into
  trouble at school or refusing
  to go to school, avoiding
  friends or siblings, thoughts
  of death or suicide

- Cognitive: difficulty
  concentrating, the decline in
  school performance, changes
  in grades
- Sleep: difficulty sleeping or
  sleeping too much
- Physical: loss of energy,
  digestive problems, changes
  in appetite, weight loss or
  gain

The symptoms can extend beyond
your mind. These eight physical
symptoms of depression prove that
depression isn't just all in your
head.

Depression causes

There are several possible causes of depression. They can range from biological to circumstantial.

Common causes include:

- Family history. You're at a higher risk for developing depression if you have a family history of depression or another mood disorder.
- Early childhood trauma. Some events impact the way that

the body reacts to fear and
stressful situations.

- Brain structure. There's a
greater risk for depression
if the frontal lobe of your
brain is less active.
However, scientists don't
know if this happens before
or after the onset of
depressive symptoms.
- Medical conditions. Certain
conditions may put you at
higher risk, such as chronic
illness, insomnia, chronic
pain, or attention-deficit
hyperactivity disorder
(ADHD).

- Drug use. A history of drug
  or alcohol misuse can impact
  your risk.

Many other people may never learn
the cause of their depression.

About 30 percent of people who
have a substance use problem also
experience depression. In
addition to these causes, other
risk factors for depression
include:

- low self-esteem or being
  self-critical
- personal history of mental
  illness
- certain medications

- stressful events, such as loss of a loved one, economic problems, or a divorce

Many factors can influence feelings of depression, as well as who develops it and who doesn't. The causes of depression are often tied to other elements of your health.

Depression test

There isn't a single test to diagnose depression. But your doctor can make a diagnosis based

on your symptoms and a
psychological evaluation.

In most cases, your doctor will
ask a series of questions about
your moods, appetite, sleep
pattern, activity level, and
thoughts.

Because depression can be linked
to other health problems, your
doctor may also conduct a
physical examination and order
blood work. Sometimes thyroid
problems or a vitamin D
deficiency can trigger symptoms
of depression.

Don't ignore symptoms of depression. If your mood doesn't improve or gets worse, seek medical help. Depression is a serious mental illness with risks of complications.

If left untreated, complications include:

- weight gain or loss
- physical pain
- substance use problems
- panic attacks
- relationship problems
- social isolation
- suicidal thoughts
- self-mutilation

Types of depression

Depression can be broken into categories depending on the severity of symptoms. Some people experience mild and temporary episodes, while others experience severe and ongoing depressive episodes.

There are two main types: major depressive disorder and persistent depressive disorder.

Major depressive disorder

Major depressive disorder is the
more severe form of depression.
It's characterized by persistent
feelings of sadness,
hopelessness, and worthlessness
that don't go away on their own.

In order to be diagnosed with
clinical depression, you must
experience 5 or more of the
following symptoms over a
two-week period:

- feeling depressed most of the
  day
- loss of interest in most
  regular activities
- significant weight loss or
  gain

- sleeping too much or not being able to sleep
- slowed thinking or movement
- fatigue or low energy most days
- feelings of worthlessness or guilt
- loss of concentration or indecisiveness
- recurring thoughts of death or suicide

There are different subtypes of major depressive disorder (which the American Psychiatric Association refers to as "specifiers"). These include:

- atypical features

- anxious distress
- mixed features
- peripartum onset, during pregnancy or right after giving birth
- seasonal patterns
- melancholic features
- psychotic features
- catatonia

Persistent depressive disorder

Persistent depressive disorder (PDD) used to be called dysthymia. It's a milder, but chronic, form of depression.

In order for the diagnosis to be made, symptoms must last for at least two years. PDD can affect your life more than major depression because it lasts for a longer period.

It's common for people with PDD to:

- lose interest in normal daily activities
- feel hopeless
- lack productivity
- have low self-esteem

Depression can be treated successfully, but it's important to stick to your treatment plan.

Treatment for depression

Living with depression can be difficult, but treatment can help improve your quality of life. Talk to your doctor about possible options.

You may successfully manage symptoms with one form of treatment, or you may find that a combination of treatments works best. It's common to combine medical treatments and lifestyle

therapies, including the
following:

Medications

Your doctor may prescribe
antidepressants, antianxiety, or
antipsychotic medications.

Each type of medication that's
used to treat depression has
benefits and potential risks.

Psychotherapy

Speaking with a therapist can
help you learn skills to cope
with negative feelings. You may

also benefit from family or group therapy sessions.

Light therapy

Exposure to doses of white light can help regulate mood and improve symptoms of depression. This therapy is commonly used in seasonal affective disorder (which is now called major depressive disorder with seasonal pattern).

Alternative therapies

Ask your doctor about acupuncture or meditation. Some herbal supplements are also used to

treat depression, like St. John's
wort, SAMe, and fish oil.

Talk with your doctor before
taking a supplement or combining
a supplement with prescription
medication because some
supplements can react with
certain medications. Some
supplements may also worsen
depression or reduce the
effectiveness of the medication.

Exercise

Aim for 30 minutes of physical
activity three to five days a
week. Exercise can increase your
body's production of endorphins,

which are hormones that improve
your mood.

Avoid alcohol and drugs

Drinking or using drugs may make
you feel better for a little bit.
But in the long run, these
substances can make depression
and anxiety symptoms worse.

Learn how to say no

Feeling overwhelmed can worsen
anxiety and depression symptoms.
Setting boundaries in your
professional and personal life
can help you feel better.

Take care of yourself

You can also improve symptoms of depression by taking care of yourself. This includes getting plenty of sleep, eating a healthy diet, avoiding negative people, and participating in enjoyable activities.

Sometimes depression doesn't respond to medication. Your doctor may recommend other treatment options if your symptoms don't improve.

These include electroconvulsive therapy, or transcranial magnetic

stimulation to treat depression
and improve your mood.

Natural treatment for depression

Traditional depression treatment
uses a combination of
prescription medication and
counselling. But there are also
alternative or complementary
treatments you can try.

It's important to remember that
many of these natural treatments
have few studies showing their

effects on depression, good or
bad. Likewise, the U.S. Food and
Drug Administration (FDA) doesn't
approve many of the dietary
supplements on the market in the
United States, so you want to
make sure you're buying products
from a trustworthy brand.

Talk to your doctor before adding
supplements to your treatment
plan.

Supplements

Several types of supplements are
thought to have some positive
impact on depression symptoms.

St. John's wort

Studies are mixed, but this natural treatment is used in Europe as antidepressant medication. In the United States, it hasn't received the same approval.

S-adenosyl-L-methionine (SAMe)

This compound has shown in limited studies to possibly ease symptoms of depression. The effects were best seen in people taking selective serotonin reuptake inhibitors (SSRIs), a type of traditional antidepressant.

5-hydroxytryptophan (5-HTP)

5-HTP may raise serotonin levels
in the brain, which could ease
symptoms. Your body makes this
chemical when you consume
tryptophan, a protein building
block.

Omega-3 fatty acids

These essential fats are
important to neurological
development and brain health.
Adding omega-3 supplements to
your diet may help reduce
depression symptoms.

Essential oils

Essential oils are a popular
natural remedy for many
conditions, but research into
their effects on depression is
limited.

People with depression may find
symptom relief with the following
essential oils:

- Wild ginger: Inhaling this
  strong scent may activate
  serotonin receptors in your
  brain. This may slow the
  release of stress-inducing
  hormones.
- Bergamot: This citrusy
  essential oil has been shown
  to reduce anxiety in patients

awaiting surgery. The same
benefit may help individuals
who experience anxiety as a
result of depression, but
there's no research to
support that claim.

Other oils, such as chamomile or
rose oil, may have a calming
effect when they're inhaled.
Those oils may be beneficial
during short-term use.

Vitamins

Vitamins are important to many
bodily functions. Research
suggests two vitamins are

especially useful for easing
symptoms of depression:

- Vitamin B: B-12 and B-6 are
  vital to brain health. When
  your vitamin B levels are
  low, your risk for developing
  depression may be higher.
- Vitamin D: Sometimes called
  the sunshine vitamin because
  exposure to the sun supplies
  it to your body, Vitamin D is
  important for brain, heart,
  and bone health. People who
  are depressed are more likely
  to have low levels of this
  vitamin.

Many herbs, supplements, and vitamins claim to help ease symptoms of depression, but most haven't shown themselves to be effective in clinical research. Learn about the ones that have shown some promise, and ask your doctor if any are right for you.

Preventing depression

Depression isn't generally considered to be preventable. It's hard to recognize what causes it, which means preventing it is more difficult.

But once you've experienced a
depressive episode, you may be
better prepared to prevent a
future episode by learning which
lifestyle changes and treatments
are helpful.

Techniques that may help include:

- regular exercise
- getting plenty of sleep
- maintaining treatments
- reducing stress
- building strong relationships
  with others

Other techniques and ideas may
also help you prevent depression.

Bipolar depression

Bipolar depression occurs in certain types of bipolar disorder, when the person experiences a depressive episode.

People with bipolar disorder may experience significant mood swings. Episodes in bipolar 2, for instance, typically range from manic episodes of high energy to depressive episodes of low energy.

This depends on the type of
bipolar disorder you have. A
diagnosis of bipolar 1 only has
to have the presence of manic
episodes, not depression.

Symptoms of depression in people
with bipolar disorder may
include:

- loss of interest or enjoyment
  from normal activities
- feeling sad, worried,
  anxious, or empty
- not having the energy or
  struggling to complete tasks
- difficulty with recall or
  memory
- sleeping too much or insomnia

- weight gain or weight loss as
  a result of increased or
  decreased appetite
- contemplating death or
  suicide

If bipolar disorder is treated,
many will experience fewer and
less severe symptoms of
depression, if they experience
depressive episodes.

Depression and anxiety

Depression and anxiety can occur
in one person at the same time.

In fact, studies have shown that 70 percent of people with depressive disorders also has anxiety symptoms.

Though they're thought to be caused by different things, depression and anxiety can produce several similar symptoms. These include irritability, difficulty with memory or concentration, and sleep problems.

The two conditions also share some common treatments. Both anxiety and depression can be treated with therapy, like cognitive behavioral therapy,

medication, or alternative
therapies, including
hypnotherapy.

If you think you're experiencing
symptoms of either or both
conditions, make an appointment
to talk with your doctor. You can
work with your doctor to identify
coexisting symptoms of anxiety
and depression and how they can
be treated.

Get Answers from a Doctor in Minutes, Anytime

Have medical questions? Connect
with a board-certified,
experienced doctor online or by
phone. Paediatricians and other
specialists available 24/7.

Depression and obsessive-compul sive disorder (OCD)

Obsessive-compulsive disorder
(OCD) is a type of anxiety
disorder. It causes unwanted and

repeated thoughts, urges, and
fears (obsessions).

These fears cause you to act out
repeated behaviors or rituals
(compulsions) that you hope will
ease the stress caused by the
obsessions.

People diagnosed with OCD
frequently find themselves in a
loop of obsessions and
compulsions. If you have these
behaviors, you may feel isolated
because of them. This can lead to
withdrawal from friends and
social situations, which can
increase your risk of depression.

It's not uncommon for someone
with OCD to also have depression.
Having one anxiety disorder can
increase your odds for having
another. Up to 80 per cent of
people with OCD also have major
depression.

This dual diagnosis is a concern
with children, too. Their
compulsive behaviors, which may
be first developing at a young
age, can make them feel unusual.
That can lead to withdrawing from
friends, and that increases the
child's risk for depression.

Depression with psychosis

Some individuals who have been diagnosed with major depression may also have symptoms of another mental disorder, psychosis. When the two conditions occur together, it's known as depressive psychosis.

Depressive psychosis causes people to see, hear, believe, or smell things that aren't real. People with the condition may also experience feelings of

sadness, hopelessness, and
irritability.

The combination of the two
conditions is particularly
dangerous. That's because someone
with depressive psychosis may
experience delusions that lead
them to be suicidal or take
unusual risks.

It's unclear what causes these
two conditions or why they can
occur together. But treatment can
successfully ease symptoms.
Treatments include medications
and electroconvulsive therapy.

Understanding the risk factors
and possible causes can help you
be aware of early symptoms.

Depression in pregnancy

Pregnancy is often an exciting
time for people. But it's still
common for an expecting mother to
experience depression.

Symptoms of depression during
pregnancy include:

- changes in appetite or eating
  habits
- feeling hopeless

- anxiety
- losing interest in activities and things you previously enjoyed
- persistent sadness
- troubles concentrating or remembering
- sleep problems, including insomnia or sleeping too much
- thoughts of death or suicide

Treatment for depression during pregnancy may focus entirely on talk therapy and other natural treatments.

While some women do take antidepressants during their pregnancy, it's not clear which

are the safest. Your doctor may
encourage you to try an
alternative option until after
the baby is delivered.

The risks for depression don't
end once the baby arrives.
Postpartum depression (currently
called major depressive disorder
with peripartum onset) is a
serious concern for new mothers.

Recognizing the symptoms may help
you spot a problem and seek help
before it becomes overwhelming.

Depression and alcohol

Research has established a link between alcohol use and depression. People who have depression are more likely to misuse alcohol.

Out of the 20.2 million U.S. adults who experienced a substance use disorder, about 50 percent had a co-occurring mental illness.

According to a 2012 study, 63.8
percent of people who are alcohol
dependent have depression.

Drinking alcohol frequently can
make symptoms of depression
worse, and people who have
depression are more likely to
misuse alcohol or become
dependent on it.

Outlook for depression

Depression can be temporary, or
it can be a long-term challenge.
Treatment doesn't always make

your depression go away
completely.

But treatment often makes
symptoms more manageable.
Managing symptoms of depression
involve finding the right
combination of medications and
therapies. If one treatment
doesn't work, you may have better
results with a different one.

Depression and Anxiety: How to Identify and Treat Coexisting Symptoms

What's the link?

Depression and anxiety can occur
at the same time. In fact, it's
been estimated that 45 percent of
people with one mental health
condition meets the criteria for
two or more disorders. One study
found that half of the people
with either anxiety or depression
have the other condition.

Although each condition has its
own causes, they may share
similar symptoms and treatments.
Read on to learn more, including
tips for management and what to
expect from a clinical diagnosis.

What are the symptoms of each condition?

Some symptoms of depression and anxiety overlaps, such as problems with sleep, irritability, and difficulty concentrating. But there are several key differences that help distinguish between the two.

Depression

Feeling down, sad, or upset is normal. It can be concerning

feeling that way for several days
or weeks on end.

Physical symptoms and behavioral
changes caused by depression
include:

- decreased energy, chronic
  fatigue, or feeling sluggish
  frequently
- difficulty concentrating,
  making decisions, or
  recalling
- pain, aches, cramps, or
  gastrointestinal problems
  without any clear cause
- changes in appetite or weight

- difficulty sleeping, waking early, or oversleeping

Emotional symptoms of depression include:

- loss of interest or no longer finding pleasure in activities or hobbies
- persistent feelings of sadness, anxiety, or emptiness
- feeling hopeless or pessimistic
- anger, irritability, or restlessness
- feeling guilty or experiencing feelings of worthlessness or helplessness

- thoughts of death or suicide
- suicide attempts

Anxiety

Anxiety, or fear and worry, can happen to anyone from time to time, too. It's not unusual to experience anxiety before a big event or important decision.

But, chronic anxiety can be debilitating and lead to irrational thoughts and fears that interfere with your daily life.

Physical symptoms and behavioral
changes caused by generalized
anxiety disorder include:

- feeling fatigued easily
- difficulty concentrating or
  recalling
- muscle tension
- racing heart
- grinding teeth
- sleep difficulties, including
  problems falling asleep and
  restless, unsatisfying sleep

Emotional symptoms of anxiety
include:

- restlessness, irritability,
  or feeling on edge

- difficulty controlling worry
  or fear
- dread
- panic

Suicide prevention

- If you think someone is at
  immediate risk of self-harm
  or hurting another person:
- • Call 911 or your local
  emergency number.
- • Stay with the person until
  help arrives.

- • Remove any guns, knives, medications, or other things that may cause harm.
- • Listen, but don't judge, argue, threaten, or yell.
- If you or someone you know is considering suicide, get help from a crisis or suicide prevention hotline. Try the National Suicide Prevention Lifeline at 800-273-8255.

A self-help test may help you

identify the
signs

You know what's normal for you. If you find yourself experiencing feelings or behaviors that aren't typical or if something seems off, this might be a sign you need to seek help from a healthcare provider. It's always better to talk about what you're feeling and experiencing so that treatment can begin early if it's necessary.

With that being said, some online self-diagnosis tests are available to help you better understand what may be happening. These tests, while helpful, aren't a replacement for a professional diagnosis from your doctor. They can't take other conditions that may be impacting your health into account, either.

Popular self-help tests for anxiety and depression include:

- depression test and anxiety test
- depression test
- anxiety test

How to manage your symptoms

In addition to a formal treatment plan from your doctor, these strategies may help you find relief from symptoms. It's important to know, though, that these tips may not work for everyone, and they may not work each time.

The goal of managing depression and anxiety is to create a series of treatment options that can all work together to help, to some degree, whenever you need to use them.

1. Allow yourself to feel what you're feeling — and know that it's not your fault

Depression and anxiety disorders are medical conditions. They aren't the result of failure or weakness. What you feel is the result of underlying causes and triggers; it's not the result of something you did or didn't do.

2. Do something that you have control over,

like making your bed or taking out the trash

At the moment, regaining a bit of control or power can help you cope with overwhelming symptoms. Accomplish a task you can manage, such as neatly restacking books or sorting your recycling. Do something to help give yourself a sense of accomplishment and power.

3. You could also create a morning, evening, or even daily routine

Routine is sometimes helpful for people with anxiety and depression. This provides structure and a sense of control. It also allows you to create space in your day for self-care techniques that can help you control symptoms.

4. Do your best to stick to a sleep schedule

Aim for seven to eight hours each night. More or less than that may complicate symptoms of both conditions. Inadequate or poor sleep can cause problems with your cardiovascular, endocrine, immune, and nervous symptoms.

5. Try to eat something nutritious, like an apple or some nuts, at least once a day

When you're feeling depressed or anxious, you may reach for comforting foods like pasta and sweets to alleviate some of the tension. However, these foods provide little nutrition. Try to help nourish your body with fruits, vegetables, lean meats, and whole grains.

6. If you're up for it, go for a walk around the block

suggests exercise can be an effective treatment for depression because it's a natural mood booster and releases feel-good hormones. However, for some people, exercise or a gym can trigger anxiety and fear. If that's the case for you, look for more natural ways to move, such as walking around your neighbourhood or looking for an online exercise video you can do at home.

7. Do something that you know brings you comfort, such as watching a favourite movie or flipping through a magazine

Give yourself time to focus on you and the things you like. Downtime is a great way to let your body rest, and it can distract your brain with things that bring you a boost.

8. If you haven't left the house in a while, consider doing something you find soothing, like getting

your nails done or getting a massage

Relaxation techniques can improve your quality of life and may reduce symptoms of depression and anxiety. Find an activity that feels right for you and you can practice regularly, such as:

- yoga
- meditation
- breathing exercises
- massage

9. Reach out to someone you're comfortable talking to and talk about whatever you feel

like, whether that's how you're feeling or something you saw on Twitter

Strong relationships are one of the best ways to help you feel better. Connecting with a friend or family member can provide a natural boost and let you find a reliable source of support and encouragement.

When to talk to your doctor

Symptoms that last two weeks or more may be an indication you

have depression, anxiety, or
both. Severe symptoms may
include:

- problems with sleep
- unexplained emotional changes
- sudden loss of interest
- feelings of worthlessness or
  helplessness

If you're not feeling like
yourself and want help
understanding, make an
appointment to see your doctor.
It's important to be open and
honest so they can fully
understand what's happening and

get a clear picture of what
you've been feeling.

Get Answers from a Doctor in Minutes, Anytime

Have medical questions? Connect
with a board-certified,
experienced doctor online or by
phone. Paediatricians and other
specialists available 24/7.

How to get a clinical diagnosis

There's no single test that can diagnose depression or anxiety. Instead, your doctor will likely conduct a physical exam and a depression or anxiety screening test. For this, they'll ask you a series of questions that help them get a better insight into what you've been experiencing.

If the results aren't clear or if your doctor suspects the symptoms may be the result of another

condition, they may order tests
to rule out underlying issues.
Blood tests can check your
thyroid, vitamin, and hormone
levels.

In some cases, general
practitioners will refer you to a
mental health expert, such as a
psychiatrist or psychologist, if
they don't feel equipped to
properly manage your symptoms and
conditions or if they suspect
you're experiencing more than one
condition.

What to expect from treatment

Although depression and anxiety are two separate conditions, they share many of the same treatments. A combination of these may be used to treat both conditions at the same time.

Therapy

Each type of therapy has unique characteristics that make it more suited to some people and not

others. Your doctor may recommend
one or more of the following:

- Cognitive behavioural therapy
  (CBT). With CBT, you'll learn
  to adjust your thoughts,
  behaviors, and reactions to
  be more even and rational.
- Interpersonal therapy. This
  type focuses on learning
  communication strategies that
  can help you express yourself
  better.
- Problem-solving therapy. This
  therapy focuses on using
  coping skills to manage
  symptoms.

Medication

Several types of medication may be used to treat depression, anxiety, or both. Because the two conditions overlap in many ways, one medication may be enough to treat both conditions. Your doctor may prescribe:

- Antidepressants. Several classes of this drug are available, including selective serotonin reuptake inhibitors (SSRIs) and serotonin-norepinephrine reuptake inhibitors (SNRIs). Each carry unique benefits and risks. The type you use will depend largely on the severity of your symptoms.

- Antianxiety medications. These drugs can help reduce symptoms of anxiety but may not help with all symptoms of depression. Some of these medications should only be used for a short amount of time due to risk of addiction.
- Mood stabilizers. These drugs may be used to stabilize mood when antidepressants don't work by themselves.

Alternative therapy

Hypnotherapy isn't widely used in psychotherapy treatments, but research suggests this alternative approach may actually help ease some symptoms of both conditions. This includes loss of focus, greater emotional control, and better management of feelings of self-consciousness.

The bottom line

You don't have to live with unusual feelings, thoughts, or other symptoms of either depression or anxiety. Talk with your doctor if these feelings or changes last longer than a week or two. Early treatment is the best way to manage the conditions and find treatments that are effective in the long-term.

Finding the right treatment for you may take some time. Most medications require two weeks or more to be effective. Likewise, you may have to try several medications to find the right option for you. Your doctor will work with you to find the best option.

Social Security Disability for Depression and Anxiety

SSDI benefits are available only to those who suffer a severe and marked impact on their lives as a result of their anxiety or depression.

Does having both clinical depression and anxiety make it any easier to get disability benefits?

Depression and anxiety can have a profound and marked impact on a person's life and career. Those who are depressed may be lethargic, disinterested in life, unmotivated, self-destructive, and even suicidal. Those who are anxious may have a hard time leaving their home or meeting people, may be unable to concentrate and may react with

extreme adverse reactions in
social and professional
situations.

Because having severe depression
or anxiety can make it impossible
for an individual to work or to
earn a living, people with both
severe depression and severe
anxiety (a common combination)
may be able to collect disability
through the Social Security
Administration's disability
insurance program (SSDI) or the
Supplemental Security Income
(SSI) program. However, to
qualify medically for SSDI or SSI

benefits on the basis of depression and anxiety, you must show Social Security that your mental condition is severe and precents you from living a normal life. For more information, see our articles on disability for depression and disability for anxiety.

If you also suffer from a physical ailment, such as heart disease, back pain, or lupus, having depression or anxiety, in addition, can sometimes make it easier to get disability benefits. For more information,

see our article on how depression
or anxiety affects a disability
claim for a physical problem.

10 Ways to Naturally Reduce Anxiety

1. Stay active

Regular exercise is good for your physical and emotional health. Regular exercise works as well as medication to ease anxiety for some people. And it's not just a short-term fix; you may experience anxiety relief for hours after working out.

2. Don't drink alcohol

Alcohol is a natural sedative. Drinking a glass of wine or a finger of whiskey when your nerves are shot may calm you at first. Once the buzz is over, however, anxiety may return with a vengeance. If you rely on alcohol to relieve anxiety instead of treating the root of the problem, you may develop alcohol dependence.

3. Stop smoking

Smokers often reach for a cigarette during stressful times. Yet, like drinking alcohol, taking a drag on a cigarette when you're stressed is a quick fix that may worsen anxiety over time. Research has shown that the earlier you start smoking in life, the higher your risk of developing an anxiety disorder later. Research also suggests nicotine and other chemicals in cigarette smoke alter pathways in the brain linked to anxiety.

4. Ditch caffeine

If you have chronic anxiety, caffeine is not your friend. Caffeine may cause nervousness and jitters, neither of which is good if you're anxious. Research has shown caffeine may cause or worsen anxiety disorders. It may also cause panic attacks in people with panic disorder. In some people, eliminating caffeine may significantly improve anxiety symptoms.

5. Get some sleep

Insomnia is a common symptom of anxiety. Make sleep a priority by:

- only sleeping at night when you're tired

- not reading or watching television in bed
- not using your phone, tablet, or computer in bed
- not tossing and turning in your bed if you can't sleep; get up and go to another room until you feel sleepy
- avoiding caffeine, large meals, and nicotine before bedtime
- keeping your room dark and cool
- writing down your worries before going to bed
- going to sleep at the same time each night

6. Meditate

A main goal of meditation is to remove chaotic thoughts from your mind and replace them with a sense of calm and mindfulness of the present moment. Meditation is known for relieving stress and anxiety. Research from John Hopkins suggests 30 minutes of daily meditation may alleviate some anxiety symptoms and act as an antidepressant.

7. Eat a healthy diet

Low blood sugar levels, dehydration, or chemicals in processed foods such as artificial flavourings, artificial colourings, and preservatives may cause mood changes in some people. A high-sugar diet may also impact

temperament. If your anxiety
worsens after eating, check your
eating habits. Stay hydrated,
eliminate processed foods, and
eat a healthy diet rich in
complex carbohydrates, fruits and
vegetables, and lean proteins.

8. Practice deep breathing

Shallow, fast breathing is common
with anxiety. It may lead to a
fast heart rate, dizziness or
lightheadedness, or even a panic
attack. Deep breathing exercises
— the deliberate process of

taking slow, even, deep breaths —
can help restore normal breathing
patterns and reduce anxiety.

9. Try aromatherapy

Aromatherapy uses fragrant
essential oils to promote health
and well-being. The oils may be
inhaled directly or added to a

warm bath or diffuser. Studies
have shown that aromatherapy:

Get Answers from a Doctor in Minutes, Anytime

Have medical questions? Connect
with a board-certified,
experienced doctor online or by
phone. Paediatricians and other
specialists available 24/7.

- helps you relax
- helps you sleep
- boosts mood

- reduces heart rate and blood
  pressure

Some essential oils used to
relieve anxiety are:

- bergamot
- lavender
- clary sage
- grapefruit
- ylang ylang

Shop online for bergamot,
lavender, clary sage, grapefruit,
and ylang-ylang essential oils.

10. Drink chamomile tea

A cup of chamomile tea is a common home remedy to calm frayed nerves and promote sleep. A 2009 study

showed chamomile may also be a powerful ally against generalized anxiety disorder. The study found people who took German chamomile capsules (220 milligrams up to five times daily) had a greater reduction in scores for tests that measure anxiety symptoms

than those who were given a
placebo.

What Triggers Anxiety? 11 Causes That May Surprise You

1. Health issues

A health diagnosis that's upsetting or difficult, such as cancer or a chronic illness, may

trigger anxiety or make it worse.
This type of trigger is very
powerful because of the immediate
and personal feelings it
produces.

You can help reduce anxiety
caused by health issues by being
proactive and engaged with your
doctor. Talking with a therapist
may also be useful, as they can
help you learn to manage your
emotions around your diagnosis.

2. Medications

Certain prescription and
over-the-counter (OTC)
medications may trigger symptoms

of anxiety. That's because active
ingredients in these medications
may make you feel uneasy or
unwell. Those feelings can set
off a series of events in your
mind and body that may lead to
additional symptoms of anxiety.

Medicines that may trigger
anxiety include:

- birth control pills
- cough and congestion
  medications
- weight loss medications

Talk with your doctor about how
these drugs make you feel and
look for an alternative that

doesn't trigger your anxiety or worsen your symptoms.

3. Caffeine

Many people rely on their morning cup of joe to wake up, but it might actually trigger or worsen anxiety. According to one study in 2010, people with panic disorder and social anxiety disorder are especially sensitive to the anxiety-inducing effects of caffeine.

Work to cut back your caffeine intake by substituting

noncaffeinated options whenever possible.

Here's a selection of decaffeinated coffee and tea to try.

4. Skipping meals

When you don't eat, your blood sugar may drop. That can lead to jittery hands and a rumbling tummy. It can also trigger anxiety.

Eating balanced meals is important for many reasons. It provides you with energy and important nutrients. If you can't

make time for three meals a day,
healthy snacks are a great way to
prevent low blood sugar, feelings
of nervousness or agitation, and
anxiety. Remember, food can
affect your mood.

5. Negative thinking

Your mind controls much of your
body, and that's certainly true
with anxiety. When you're upset
or frustrated, the words you say
to yourself can trigger greater
feelings of anxiety.

If you tend to use a lot of
negative words when thinking
about yourself, learning to

refocus your language and
feelings when you start down this
path is helpful. Working with a
therapist can be incredibly
helpful in this process.

6. Financial concerns

Worries about saving money or
having debt can trigger anxiety.
Unexpected bills or money fears
are triggers, too.

Learning to manage these types of
triggers may require seeking
professional help, such as from a
financial advisor. Feeling you
have a companion and a guide in

the process may ease your
concern.

7. Parties or social events

If a room full of strangers
doesn't sound like fun, you're
not alone. Events that require
you to make small talk or
interact with people you don't
know can trigger feelings of
anxiety, which may be diagnosed
as a social anxiety disorder.

To help ease your worries or
unease, you can always bring
along a companion when possible.
But it's also important to work

with a professional to find
coping mechanisms that make these
events more manageable in the
long term.

8. Conflict

Relationship problems, arguments,
disagreements — these conflicts
can all trigger or worsen
anxiety. If conflict particularly
triggers you, you may need to
learn conflict resolution
strategies. Also, talk with a
therapist or other mental health
expert to learn how to manage the
feelings these conflicts cause.

9. Stress

Daily stressors like traffic jams or missing your train can cause anyone anxiety. But long-term or chronic stress can lead to long-term anxiety and worsening symptoms, as well as other health problems.

Stress can also lead to behaviors like skipping meals, drinking alcohol, or not getting enough sleep. These factors can trigger or worsen anxiety, too.

Treating and preventing stress often requires learning coping mechanisms. A therapist or counselor can help you learn to recognize your sources of stress and handle them when they become overwhelming or problematic.

10. Public events or performances

Public speaking, talking in front of your boss, performing in a competition, or even just reading aloud is a common trigger of anxiety. If your job or hobbies require this, your doctor or therapist can work with you to learn ways to be more comfortable in these settings.

Also, positive reinforcements from friends and colleagues can help you feel more comfortable and confident.

11. Personal triggers

These triggers may be difficult to identify, but a mental health specialist is trained to help you identify them. These may begin with a smell, a place, or even a song. Personal triggers remind you, either consciously or unconsciously, of bad memory or traumatic event in your life. Individuals with post-traumatic stress disorder (PTSD) frequently experience anxiety triggers from environmental triggers.

Identifying personal triggers may take time, but it's important so you can learn to overcome them.

Tips for identifying triggers

If you can identify and understand your triggers, you can work to avoid them and to cope. You can learn specific coping

strategies to handle the triggers
when they happen.

Here are three tips for
identifying triggers:

- Start a journal. Write down
  when your anxiety is
  noticeable and record what
  you think might have led to
  the trigger. Some apps can
  help you track your anxiety,
  too.
- Work with a therapist. Some
  anxiety triggers can be
  difficult to identify, but a
  mental health specialist has
  training that can help you.
  They may use talk therapy,

journaling, or other methods
to find triggers.

- Be honest with yourself.
  Anxiety can cause negative
  thoughts and poor
  self-assessments. This can
  make identifying triggers
  difficult because of anxious
  reactions. Be patient with
  yourself and be willing to
  explore things in your past
  to identify how they may
  affect you today.

Symptoms of anxiety

The most common symptoms of
anxiety include:

- uncontrollable worry
- fear
- muscle tension
- a fast heartbeat
- difficulty sleeping or
  insomnia
- difficulty concentrating
- physical discomfort
- tingling
- restlessness
- feeling on edge
- irritability

If you experience these symptoms
regularly for six months or more,
you may have a generalized

anxiety disorder (GAD). Other
types of anxiety disorders exist
as well. The symptoms for those
may be different than GAD. For
example, with the panic disorder
you may experience:

- a rapid heartbeat or
  palpitations
- sweating
- trembling
- shaking
- feeling as if your throat is
  closing

Can Anxiety Kill You?

Panic attacks can be one of the scariest experiences to go through. The attacks can range from a sudden surge of fear that only lasts a few minutes to heart palpitations and shortness of breath that mimic a heart attack.

But it's not just the symptoms that make panic attacks so

debilitating. It's also the feeling of being out of control. Not knowing why you're having one — or when an attack might strike next — can make daily tasks a challenge.

If you are experiencing panic attacks, you may have a type of anxiety disorder called panic disorder. It is estimated that almost 5 percent of American adults will experience panic disorder at some point in their lives.

The good news is that there are steps you can take to help lessen the severity of the attacks.

Plus, the long-term treatments
available for managing anxiety
and panic attacks are promising.

What are the symptoms of a panic attack?

Symptoms of a panic attack can
vary from person to person and
even from attack to attack.
Celeste Viciere, LMHC, who
provides cognitive behavioral
therapy, says that's why panic
attacks can be tricky: when
people describe a panic attack to
her, they often say: "It felt

like I was having a heart attack, and I couldn't breathe." However, everyone can experience different symptoms.

Most panic attacks last less than 30 minutes — with the average lasting around 10 minutes — although some of the symptoms may last a lot longer. During this time, you may experience a need to flee until the attack is over.

Although the average length of a panic attack may not seem like a long time, for the person experiencing a full-blown attack, it can feel like an eternity.

So how can you identify if you
are having a panic attack?

The following list of symptoms
may be your first indication that
you are experiencing an attack:

- sweating
- nausea
- chest pains and feeling weak,
  like you are going to
  collapse
- hyperventilating
- shortness of breath (many
  people experience this as
  hyperventilation; some people
  also experience a choking
  sensation)

- heart palpitations and chest pain
- trembling or shaking
- sweating
- feeling detached from your settings and dizzy
- numbness or tingling sensation

What can you do during a panic attack to make it stop?

When you are in a full-blown panic attack, it can be

challenging to stop it. Viciere
says the reason why it feels so
difficult is that the physical
symptoms actually cause you to
panic even more.

If you have ruled out other
medical diagnoses, and your
doctor has confirmed that you are
having panic attacks, Viciere
says to try and be intentional in
telling yourself that you are
going to be okay.

"Your mind can play tricks on
you, and it can feel like you are
dying because of the physical
symptoms, but if you tell
yourself you are going to be

okay, it can help to calm
yourself down," she explains.

When you are experiencing a panic
attack, she suggests you work on
slowing down your breaths. You
can do this by counting backward
and taking slow, deep breaths.

During the attack, your breaths
will feel shallow, and it may
feel like you are running out of
air. That's why Viciere suggests
these steps:

- Start by breathing in.
- As you are breathing in,
  count in your head (or out
  loud) for about 6 seconds to

make your in-breath last
longer.

- It's also important that you
breathe through your nose.
- Then breathe out for about 7
to 8 seconds.
- Repeat this method a few
times during the attack.

In addition to breathing
exercises, you can also practice
relaxation techniques. Focusing
as much energy as possible on
getting your body to relax is
essential.

Some people find success by
regularly practicing yoga,
meditation, and breathing

exercises when they are not
having a panic attack. This helps
them access these techniques more
quickly during an attack.

What are some of the long-term treatments?

Get Answers from a Doctor in Minutes, Anytime

Have medical questions? Connect
with a board-certified,

experienced doctor online or by phone. Pediatricians and other specialists available 24/7.

There are many ways to treat panic disorder and panic attacks including CBT (psychotherapy), exposure therapy, and medications.

Otherwise known as "talk therapy," psychotherapy can help you understand your diagnosis and how it impacts your life. Your therapist will also work with you to develop strategies that help decrease the severity of the symptoms.

One psychotherapy technique that has been proven successful in treating panic disorder and attacks is CBT. This form of therapy emphasizes the important role that thinking has in how we feel and what we do.

CBT teaches you new ways of thinking, acting, and reacting to situations that cause anxiety. It also teaches you how to view panic attacks differently and demonstrates ways to reduce anxiety. Plus, you can learn how to change unhealthy thoughts and behaviors that bring on panic attacks.

But if therapy isn't something
you can access, Viciere
recommends the following
activities to help you get a
better understanding of your
triggers:

- Journal your feelings. Write
  down the times when you find
  yourself feeling overwhelmed
  and anxious.
- Journal your thoughts. Since
  most of us deal with negative
  thoughts we may not even be
  aware of, it can be helpful
  to write these thoughts down.
  This can help you begin to
  understand how your inner

thoughts play a role in your
mindset.

- Daily breathing exercises.
  Another helpful technique is
  to work on breathing
  exercises daily, even when
  you don't have a panic
  attack. When you're more in
  sync with your breaths, you
  can become more self-aware of
  when you are not taking them.

Even though panic attacks can
feel like a heart attack or other
serious condition, it will not
cause you to die. However, panic
attacks are serious and need to
be treated.

If you find yourself experiencing
any of these symptoms on a
regular basis, it's essential
that you contact your physician
for further help.